A Webs to Whales
Nature Tale

TRUE BLUE FRIEND

written by Cheryl Block
illustrated by Gene Takeshita
multi-media by Jeff Reynolds

Block Publishing
*Building a foundation for learning
one block at a time*

© 2006 Block Publishing
All rights reserved
www.blockpub.com
ISBN 0-9761625-2-0
Printed in Canada

"Watch this!" the young humpback cried, as he again leaped high into the air.

But his friends had gotten tired of
watching him and were heading off to play.
"That's okay," thought the little humpback.
"I'll just play by myself."

He continued to breach, lifting high out of the water and spinning, his flippers sticking out like wings.

When he finally looked up, he saw that he was a long way from the other whales. He could see only a spout in the distance.

He noticed a fishing boat nearby. Curious, the little humpback swam closer.

Rolling on one side, he waved his flipper in the air. He could see someone standing on the boat.

The little whale couldn't resist showing off. He shot up in the air and landed with a huge splash. This was fun!

"Go back to your mother, young whale,"
a deep voice rumbled. Startled, the young whale
turned and saw an old blue whale behind him.

The little whale had seen the old blue whale only from a distance. The old blue always stayed by himself.

The old blue whale had lived a very long time. He still remembered the whaling boats and men with harpoons. This little humpback reminded him of himself as a young whale, always looking for adventure.

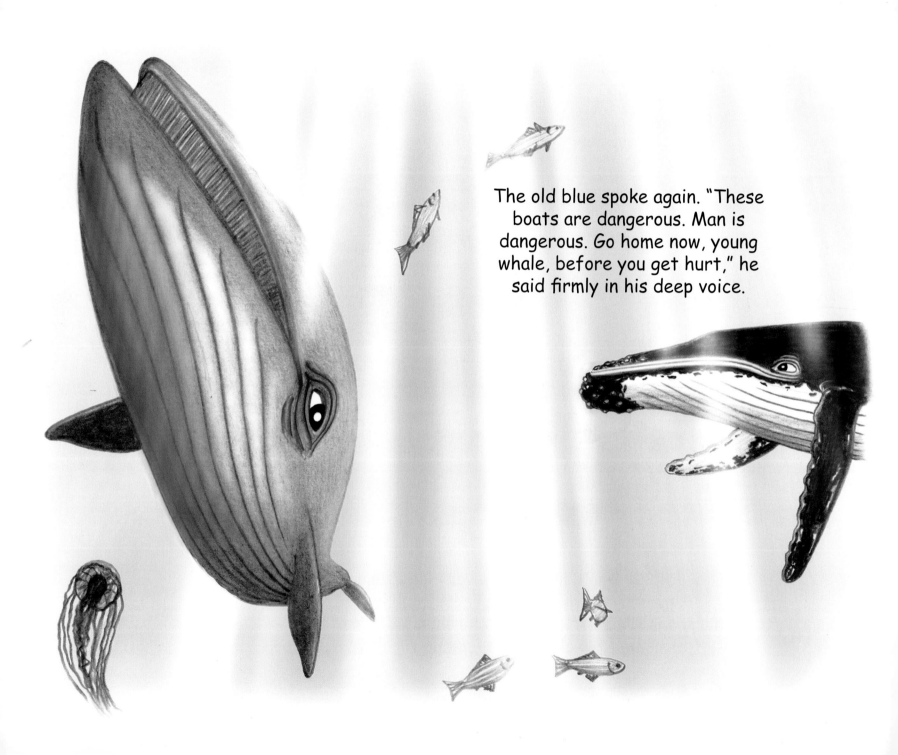

The old blue spoke again. "These boats are dangerous. Man is dangerous. Go home now, young whale, before you get hurt," he said firmly in his deep voice.

The little humpback started back towards his friends. "I don't see anything to make me afraid," he thought. "The blue whale is just old." He started to speak up, but when he looked back, the old blue was gone.

The little whale's mother scolded him for wandering off and warned him about going near boats. For awhile, the little humpback stayed close to the other whales.

But when he saw a fishing boat
in the distance, he got curious again.
He had forgotten all about the warnings.
None of his friends would go with him,
so he went on his own.

When he reached the boat, he began to slap the water with his flipper. As he swam near the boat, he spotted a large school of fish circling beneath him. He dove down to take a closer look.

The fish were swirling all about him.
As he chased after them, the little
whale didn't notice the huge net
slowly surrounding them.

When he turned to swim back to the other whales, he sensed something in front of him. Was this a net? He remembered hearing the older whales talk about whales that had become trapped in nets. He pushed against the net, but it wouldn't break.

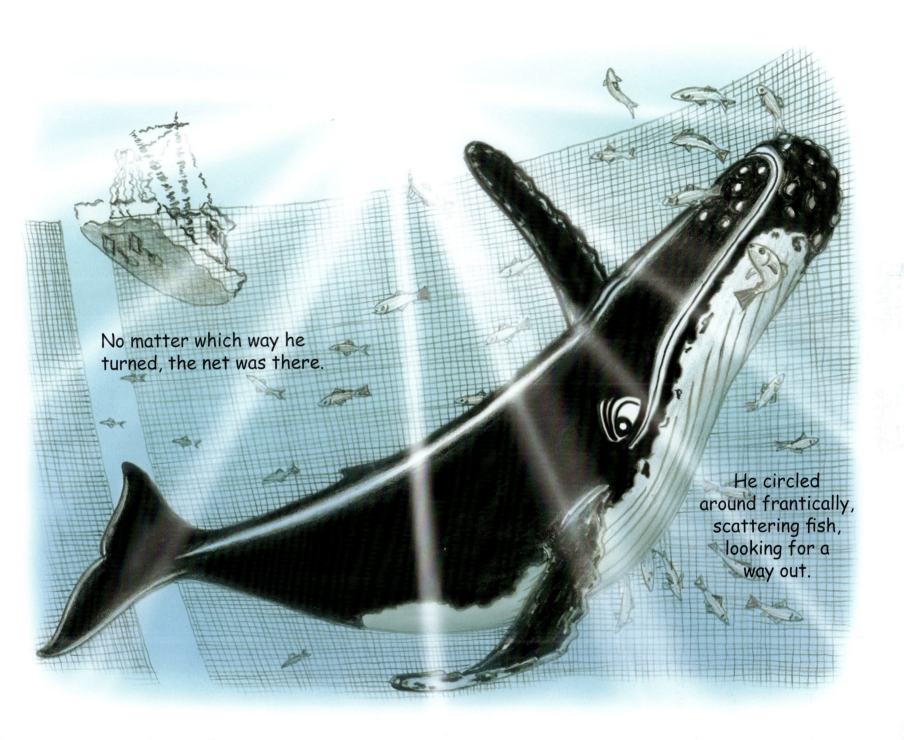

No matter which way he turned, the net was there.

He circled around frantically, scattering fish, looking for a way out.

Frightened now, the little whale called out for his mother. But his voice was too small, and she was too far away. The little humpback swam back and forth inside the ever-tightening net.

"I'm here, little whale," said a low, rumbling voice. It was the old blue whale! The little humpback rushed towards him. "Stay back from the net or you'll get tangled," he warned. The little whale moved back, watching hopefully.

Circling back and forth, the old blue looked for a way to free the little whale. He soon realized that only the men could release the little whale from the net. Somehow, the old blue must show them what was happening.

Gathering speed, the old whale suddenly lifted his huge body out of the water in front of the fishing boat, breaching the surface. He landed heavily, sending a great wave of water onto the boat. The amazed fishermen raced to the side of the boat. Rarely had they seen such a sight. What could have caused the blue to breach?

Looking about for a reason, they spotted the young humpback inside the net and realized he was trapped. The men quickly let the bottom of the net open so the little whale could swim out.

Seeing the opening, the young whale
dove out and raced away from the boat.
He looked about for the blue whale.
As he started to head back towards
his mother, the blue whale appeared.

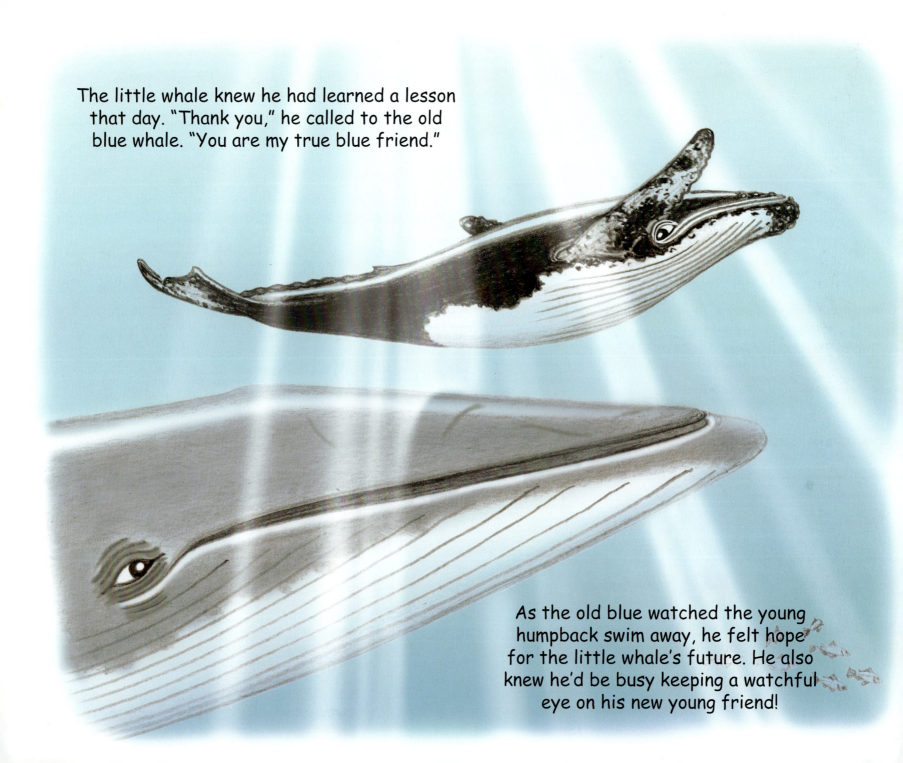

The little whale knew he had learned a lesson that day. "Thank you," he called to the old blue whale. "You are my true blue friend."

As the old blue watched the young humpback swim away, he felt hope for the little whale's future. He also knew he'd be busy keeping a watchful eye on his new young friend!